In all the things you do,

Don't Forget U! 🤍

Hey, you!

I am thrilled you have decided to take your vision on a journey this year. I have no objections to vision boards, but someone is eagerly waiting to benefit from the fruit of your dreams. This book is just my way of helping the cultivation process.

I understand that transformation can be scary. However, standing still should frighten you even more. It is completely normal to feel anxious about change, but we still have to find the courage to navigate roads that are paved with insecurities and imperfections to arrive at better versions of ourselves.

Your vision is waiting, so let's get to work!

Xo, LaShon

"I praise you because you made me in an amazing and wonderful way. What you have done is wonderful."   Psalms 139:14

"If you set goals and go after them with all the determination you can muster, your gifts will take you places that will amaze you." — Les Brown

Don't Forget to Be Amazing This Year!

I conclude most of my emails, text messages, and phone calls with the powerful reminder— "Don't Forget to Be Amazing!" This is not just a casual sign-off; it is a deliberate choice with a profound purpose. What's my why? Because commonly, there's an amazing woman on the other end of that communication. I say it to let her know that I see her strength and value, as we frequently feel overlooked and unsupported. Words are powerful, so reminding her to be amazing is my way of infusing positivity into her day.

Additionally, we all crave significance. Yet, the needs and aspirations of many women get lost behind the demands and expectations of those around us. We spend our days juggling roles as daughters, sisters, friends, and, most importantly, as wives and mothers, bearing the lion's share of parenting and household responsibilities. We are expected to be "all things to all people" while striving for success and grasping for the elusive concept of work-life balance, whatever that may be.

We strive to master multitasking, but when our humanity reveals itself, and we cannot be everything to everyone, we carry the weight of that guilt as well. Rarely do we grant ourselves the grace that we willingly bestow on others when they fall short, so we perpetually find ourselves coming in last place in our own lives.

Despite your busy schedule, reclaim some of your time and invest it in yourself with this project. Don't worry it will not be labor-intensive. It is a labor of love. You are not bound by dates, but a new year offers an opportune time to start. Our weeks already seem to blend into a seamless continuum; months blur from one holiday to the next, and years pass by quicker than the shock on our faces. So, now is the perfect time to be intentional on purpose and treat your time as the precious currency that it is.

"Don't Forget to Be Amazing This Year" was born during the pandemic, when I had a surplus of time. The world was shrouded in uncertainty, which forced me to focus on the few things I could still control. With most of us confined to our homes, my primary goal became to preserve my physical, spiritual, and mental well-being. My living room transformed into a makeshift gym, virtual services became my spiritual sanctuary, and I became deliberate about limiting my media consumption since news related to the pandemic was very terrifying during that time.

But despite filling my days with exercise, books, and sermons by Bishop T.D. Jakes and the teachings of Dr. Dharius Daniels, I still found myself with ample amounts of alone time. During the quarantine-induced isolation, I experienced a kind of solitude that was different from the one I sought in the past. This time, I was forced to be alone by something that I couldn't even see.

Being coerced into anything is never a pleasant feeling, and the fear and uncertainty that came along with it really tested my faith back then. But I eventually realized that if we knew the outcome of every situation, there would be no need for faith. So, as the world sowed seeds of doubt, I continued to safeguard both my mental and physical health, ultimately cultivating a newfound strength and resilience.

I was not alone in this experience since your life was likely upended, too. The pandemic touched everyone differently, and we all had to adapt to a new normal. We quickly modified our lives because we had no other option. That experience proves you can make necessary changes in your life when that is the only choice that you have. So, if you can adjust to circumstances beyond your control, when will you develop the courage to change what you can?

"Don't Forget to Be Amazing This Year" is just here to help you answer that question. Refocus on yourself with this book and prioritize your own goals. Use it as a tool to be a better steward of your time, temple, and talent. It offers more guidance than a vision board because it includes a compass designed by someone you should trust...you! It offers different strategies and weekly exercises to be completed over the course of a year because life is a journey, not just a destination.

Be prepared to assess and challenge yourself, and at the close of each month, you will engage in reflection. It's important to not only expect support and motivation but to also be accountable for your actions and decisions. Keep this in mind, being average is easy, but being amazing takes effort!

Take care, and don't forget to be amazing this year!

xo. LaShon Fryer

Affirmations

Before you start, I need a little positive self-talk and commitment!

Repeat the following:

- I promise to keep moving forward even as butterflies take flight in my stomach, leaving a trail of fear.

- I will approach this project with intention and realistic time expectations.

- I promise that I will not be affected by the opinions of people who are not in the arena with me.

Print name:

- I promise to find peace during the ebbs and flows of change by accepting the things that I cannot change.

- I promise to make being amazing a daily habit.

Signature_____

Date_____

Self Reflection

Coming
Up...

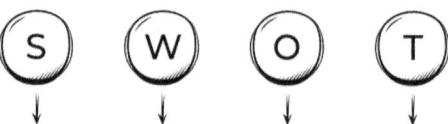

Self-improvement books often begin with a wheel of life, yet my approach is different. Drawing from my MBA background, I tend to see problems through a business lens. However, two decades of experience working with diverse individuals and families has given me a "Ph.D. in Hard Knocks," which keeps my lens focused on humanity.

When I combine my education with my experience, my preferred focus is self-sufficiency and social ills. One effective way that I have helped individuals overcome obstacles in their lives is by conducting a personal SWOT analysis, which is a strategic approach to self-improvement.

The acronym SWOT (Strengths, Weaknesses, Opportunities, and Threats) is commonly used in business to identify strategies and growth opportunities through collaborative brainstorming. However, you can also use this method for personal self-assessment. It involves evaluating your strengths, weaknesses, opportunities, and threats from your own perspective. You can also ask people you trust for their honest feedback on specific sections.

The Why of It All

Completing a self-assessment is a very productive way to inspect yourself and evaluate if you are progressing or regressing. And even if you discover that you are not living in alignment with your current vision and goals, the SWOT is a great tool to help you identify your gaps.

Strength Questions

Do not be modest in this section, this is your opportunity to be that GIRL!

What are my gifts and innate talents that I excel at without much effort?

- _____
- _____
- _____
- _____

When did I discover that these were gifts?

- _____
- _____
- _____
- _____

How have they contributed to my biggest accomplishments?

- _____
- _____
- _____
- _____

How can I use these strengths to help me with my weaknesses?

- _____
- _____
- _____
- _____

Weakness Questions

Women are often their own worst critics. Don't be too hard on yourself in this section, as we all have areas to improve. Be honest without being harsh.

What tasks or activities do I find challenging? Why?

- _____
- _____
- _____
- _____

Do I have any specific areas where I often receive constructive criticism?

- _____
- _____
- _____
- _____

Have I been unable to achieve specific goals due to this weakness?

- _____
- _____
- _____
- _____

What habits or behaviors can I change to transform this weakness into a strength?

- _____
- _____
- _____
- _____

Opportunity questions will vary according to the season you're currently in. That's why I've included four different options. According to a recent Forbes article, the most popular New resolutions for individuals aged 26-57 are improving mental health, physical health (fitness/losing weight), and finances. Therefore, this section's prompt questions will focus on mental health, fitness, and finances. However, I've also included career-related questions since I pivoted slightly last year, and you may be doing the same.

*Notes: Davis, S. (2023, May 09). New Year's Resolutions Statistics 2023. https://www.forbes.com/health/mind/new-years-resolutions-statistics/

Opportunity Questions

Mental Health

What are some steps that I can take right now to improve my mental health?

- _____
- _____
- _____
- _____

What triggers or patterns of behavior can I try to avoid to improve my mental health?

- _____
- _____
- _____
- _____

What do I believe my barriers are between me and achieving better mental health?

- _____
- _____
- _____
- _____

Should I seek assistance from a therapist or my support network to improve my mental health?

- _____
- _____
- _____
- _____

Opportunity Questions

Physical Health

What physical activity or exercise can be incorporated into my weekly routine?

- _____
- _____
- _____
- _____

What lifestyle changes can I adopt to improve my diet?

- _____
- _____
- _____
- _____

What can I do to manage stress in a healthier way besides emotional eating or not eating at all?

- _____
- _____
- _____
- _____

Who or what can become my accountability partner?

- _____
- _____
- _____
- _____

Opportunity Questions

Financial Health

What financial tools or resources can I start using to help manage my finances?

- _____
- _____
- _____
- _____

What are some specific financial challenges that I can address during this process to improve my financial health?

- _____
- _____
- _____
- _____

What unnecessary expenses can I delete or cut back on to save additional money?

- _____
- _____
- _____
- _____

What do I need to unlearn to improve my money story?

- _____
- _____
- _____
- _____

Opportunity Questions

Career Health

What are some areas of interest and passion that I can pursue this season?

- _____
- _____
- _____
- _____

What emerging trends in technologies can I learn more about?

- _____
- _____
- _____
- _____

What areas of personal development should I focus on in my current season?

- _____
- _____
- _____
- _____

How can I expand my network or connections to create new opportunities?

- _____
- _____
- _____
- _____

Threat Questions

What bad habits prevent me from reaching my goals?

- _____
- _____
- _____
- _____

What is an obstacle that is unclear or uncertain and is preventing me from reaching my goals?

- _____
- _____
- _____
- _____

Does technology threaten my current career choice?

- _____
- _____
- _____
- _____

Is my current circle helping or hurting me?

- _____
- _____
- _____
- _____

Your SWOT analysis may vary significantly from the ones I mentioned earlier because you could be in a different season of life. But don't worry, since this journey is entirely yours, you can adjust it accordingly to suit your needs. If you need additional resources, you can visit my website: dontforgetyou.com.

Write the Vision and Make It Plain

Before you start your vision exercise on the next page, I want to explain why writing your vision down on paper is important. When you physically write your vision down, it becomes tangible, and you can add details for clarity. This will help you use your senses to bring your dreams to reality. Once you put pen to paper, you cannot unsee it, and your goals will move to the forefront of your mind instead of getting lost in other thoughts. By perceiving your intentions, you become committed to them and will be accountable to yourself.

Your Vision

_____

_____

_____

_____

_____

_____

_____

_____

_____

_____

_____

_____

_____

_____

_____

_____

HABAKKUK 2:2-3 NIV

○ *Fitness*

○ *Finances*

○ *Faith*

○ *Focus*

Make it
Amazing
Vision Board

Notes :

_____

_____

_____

_____

_____

_____ ○ ○ ○ ○

○ *Fun*

○ *Family*

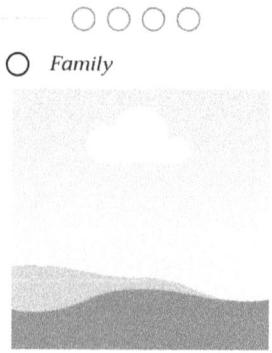

○ *Friends*

The Science Behind Visualization

Writing down our vision on paper is a form of visualization. It is not just about creating a colorful poster board to affirm our dreams and goals. The science behind visualization lies in how our brains process information. According to neuroscience, when we visualize something, we activate the same neural pathways as when we accomplish something. By creating a vivid mental picture, we engage our senses and imagine what the experience feels like, and our brain believes that we have already experienced it.

The amygdala, a small but significant part of our brain that is responsible for our emotions, assesses how important a goal is to us. The frontal lobe, responsible for decision-making, planning, and problem-solving, collaborates with the amygdala to help us focus on moving toward the environments, activities, and skill sets that align with our desired outcomes. This also means that we become less interested in being around people and environments that do not support our goals.

Our brains have neuroplasticity, meaning our experiences and outside stimuli can reshape our brains. This is what happens when we set goals. A study conducted at the University of Texas showed that goal-setting helped female patients with MS to make behavior changes.

Visualization is an excellent tool to have in our goal toolbox. However, when discussing visualization, some self-help books and coaches fail to emphasize the need to also visualize the work and action steps required to achieve goals. For example, when trying to lose weight, visualizing oneself at their goal weight is not enough. It is also important to incorporate images of healthy eating, regular exercise, and lifestyle changes. Visualization is like practice; completing the steps needed to reach our goals is the game.

*Notes: Stuifbergen, A. K., Becker, H., Timmerman, G. M., & Kullberg, V. (2003). The use of individualized goal setting to facilitate behavior change in women with multiple sclerosis. https://doi.org/10.1097/01376517-200304000-00005

Be Amazing On Purpose!

Every day is a new blessing, and we receive new mercies every morning. Therefore, we should be amazing on purpose. Being intentional with our time helps us to focus on our daily tasks and stay committed to our weekly goals. We should also give ourselves grace when things don't go according to plan or purpose. Just remember, we are only seeking progress—not perfection.

The **AMAZING** Approach

Please note that there are seven questions in total for each week of the year. Ideally, you should aim to answer the first question on Monday, the second on Tuesday, the third on Wednesday, and so on. However, this is your compass, so you complete the questions on whatever day you wish.

Accomplish: what do you want to accomplish this week?

Measure: how are you going to measure your accomplishment(s)?

Accountability: how will you hold yourself accountable?

Zen-Zone: don't forget your zen.

Information: what additional information or resources do you need to get to your next step?

Noteworthy: what happened this week that warrants a journal entry?

Gratitude: what are you most grateful for today?

"Yesterday is gone. Tomorrow has not yet come. We have only today. Let us begin." — Mother Teresa.

Week 1

ACCOMPLISH, WHAT DO YOU WANT TO ACCOMPLISH THIS WEEK?

_____

_____

_____

_____

MEASURE, HOW ARE YOU GOING TO MEASURE YOUR ACCOMPLISHMENT(S)?

_____

_____

_____

_____

ACCOUNTABILITY, HOW WILL YOU HOLD YOURSELF ACCOUNTABLE?

_____

_____

_____

_____

ZEN-ZONE, DON'T FORGET YOUR ZEN.

_____

_____

_____

_____

Week 1

INFORMATION, WHAT ADDITIONAL INFORMATION OR RESOURCES DO YOU NEED TO GET TO YOUR NEXT STEP?

_____

_____

_____

_____

NOTEWORTHY, WHAT HAPPENED THIS WEEK THAT WARRANTS A JOURNAL ENTRY?

_____

_____

_____

_____

GRATITUDE, WHAT ARE YOU MOST GRATEFUL FOR TODAY?

_____

_____

_____

_____

"The only thing worse than being blind is having sight but no vision." —Helen Keller

Week 2

ACCOMPLISH, WHAT DO YOU WANT TO ACCOMPLISH THIS WEEK?

_____

_____

_____

_____

MEASURE, HOW ARE YOU GOING TO MEASURE YOUR ACCOMPLISHMENT(S)?

_____

_____

_____

_____

ACCOUNTABILITY, HOW WILL YOU HOLD YOURSELF ACCOUNTABLE?

_____

_____

_____

_____

ZEN-ZONE, DON'T FORGET YOUR ZEN.

_____

_____

_____

_____

Week 2

INFORMATION, WHAT ADDITIONAL INFORMATION OR RESOURCES DO YOU NEED TO GET TO YOUR NEXT STEP?

_____

_____

_____

_____

NOTEWORTHY, WHAT HAPPENED THIS WEEK THAT WARRANTS A JOURNAL ENTRY?

_____

_____

_____

_____

GRATITUDE, WHAT ARE YOU MOST GRATEFUL FOR TODAY?

_____

_____

_____

_____

"The measure of intelligence is the ability to change."
—Albert Einstein

"Embrace what you don't know especially in the beginning, because what you don't know can become your greatest asset."—Sara Blakely

Our mindset is the lens through which we perceive the world, but it is blurred with our biases. We all develop belief-based experiences, which shape our attitudes towards ourselves, our intelligence, and the world. While this can help us filter information and set expectations, it can also make us feel inadequate.

It is common to describe people as having either a growth or a fixed mindset. These terms were coined by the renowned psychologist Carol S. Dweck, Ph.D. In her book, "Mindset," she explains that having a fixed mindset means believing that intelligence, personality, and moral character are "carved in stone." Meanwhile, believing that you can develop your qualities through hard work and support from others is having a growth mindset. Although both terms are accurate, I personally refer to a fixed mindset as a poverty mindset and a growth mindset as a prosperity mindset.

During my professional journey, I have worked with numerous individuals and families who were considered less fortunate. For some of them, living in scarcity has become their norm, and they cannot envision a life beyond their current circumstances. Meanwhile, others show remarkable resilience in the face of adversity because they believe that they have the power to change their current situation.

A poverty mindset focuses solely on obstacles, while a prosperity mindset sees obstacles as opportunities. Fortunately, our brains have the ability to unlearn some of our fixed beliefs when we are exposed to new experiences and different perspectives. To transition from poverty to prosperity, we need to learn what we need to fix.

We evolve every day, so mindset shifts are a continuous part of life. However, here are some steps that can help with these transitions:

- **Challenge your beliefs**. If you hold certain beliefs about yourself that you consider to be absolute truths and they hinder you from trying new things, then you have limiting beliefs. Whenever I need to challenge my own limiting beliefs, I examine the thoughts by testing them with facts. Suppose that someone believed that becoming successful required a degree. That thought could be challenged with numerous examples. For instance, Ralph Lauren grew up in a poor neighborhood and dropped out of college after two years, yet he still managed to become successful. Jay-Z, who is now a billionaire, did not receive any formal education. Janice Bryant Howroyd, one of the most successful women in America, started her own company, the Act One Group, with just $900 when she moved to L.A. These are people that you may recognize or whom you can research. However, take some time to think of your own examples that can easily disprove the limiting thoughts you have of yourself.

- **Challenge yourself**: Many of us have fears that stem from the worry that we might not meet expectations or that we may end up looking foolish. However, to overcome our fears, we should actively seek out challenges and use them as opportunities for personal growth rather than seeing them as threats. When faced with a challenging situation, I tend to take a worst-case-scenario approach. Identify the worst outcome and also a contingency plan to deal with it. So, even if it becomes a reality, you'll be okay. Alternatively, I also like to imagine the best-case scenario to help me stay optimistic and motivated. Throughout this process, I ensure that I maintain a balanced perspective.

- **Challenge your perspective**. Being open to hearing different opinions and ideas is important. Everyone has their own unique perspective, but considering different points of view can lead to a more open mind.

Notes: Dweck, C.S. (2008). Mindset. Ballantine Books.

- **Challenge what you say to yourself.** Combat negative thoughts with affirmations since negative and positive thoughts cannot coexist. I tend to be my own worst critic, but then I was trained to never say anything to myself that I wouldn't say to another person. Words are powerful, so be intentional in how you think and speak. Keep it cute, or keep it mute!

If you would like to take a self-assessment to be able to recognize your "fixed" areas, there is a free assessment on the following page.

Mindset Assessment

1. I believe that my abilities are fixed and cannot be significantly improved.

Strongly agree **Agree** **Disagree** **Strongly Disagree**

2. I enjoy taking on new challenges, even if they initially seem difficult.

Strongly agree **Agree** **Disagree** **Strongly Disagree**

3. I see effort as a road to mastery and improvement.

Strongly agree **Agree** **Disagree** **Strongly Disagree**

4. When I face obstacles, I tend to give up easily.

Strongly agree **Agree** **Disagree** **Strongly Disagree**

5. I believe I can develop any skill with discipline and hard work.

Strongly agree **Agree** **Disagree** **Strongly Disagree**

6. I often seek feedback from others I trust to improve my performance.

Strongly agree **Agree** **Disagree** **Strongly Disagree**

Continue on the next page

7. I avoid challenges I'm not confident I'll excel in.

Strongly agree   **Agree**   **Disagree**   **Strongly Disagree**

8. I feel threatened by the success and achievements of other people.

Strongly agree   **Agree**   **Disagree**   **Strongly Disagree**

9. Talent alone is sufficient for success.

Strongly agree   **Agree**   **Disagree**   **Strongly Disagree**

10. I find inspiration in the success of others and use it to motivate myself to improve.

Strongly agree   **Agree**   **Disagree**   **Strongly Disagree**

How to Score the Assessment

For questions 1, 4, 7, 8, and 9, assign 3 points for "Strongly Agree," 2 points for "Agree," 1 point for "Disagree", and 0 points for "Strongly Disagree."

For questions 2, 3, 5, 6, and 10, assign 0 points for "Strongly Agree," 1 point for "Agree", 2 points for "Disagree", and 3 points for "Strongly Disagree."

Your Results:
0-10 points: Strong indication of a growth mindset.
11-20 points: A mix of growth and fixed mindset beliefs.
21-30 points: Strong indication of a fixed mindset.

FYI: This assessment is a general suggestion and should not be the only tool used to determine your mindset. For additional assessment resources, visit dontforgetu.com.

"Twenty years from now you will be more disappointed
by the things you did not do than by the ones you did."
– Mark Twain

Week 3

ACCOMPLISH, WHAT DO YOU WANT TO ACCOMPLISH THIS WEEK?

_____

_____

_____

_____

MEASURE, HOW ARE YOU GOING TO MEASURE YOUR ACCOMPLISHMENT(S)?

_____

_____

_____

_____

ACCOUNTABILITY, HOW WILL YOU HOLD YOURSELF ACCOUNTABLE?

_____

_____

_____

_____

ZEN-ZONE, DON'T FORGET YOUR ZEN.

_____

_____

_____

_____

Week 3

INFORMATION, WHAT ADDITIONAL INFORMATION OR RESOURCES DO YOU NEED TO GET TO YOUR NEXT STEP?

_____
_____
_____
_____

NOTEWORTHY, WHAT HAPPENED THIS WEEK THAT WARRANTS A JOURNAL ENTRY?

_____
_____
_____
_____

GRATITUDE, WHAT ARE YOU MOST GRATEFUL FOR TODAY?

_____
_____
_____
_____

We never stop to consider that our beliefs are only a relative truth that's always going to be distorted by all the knowledge we have stored in our memory."—Don Miguel Ruiz

Week 4

ACCOMPLISH, WHAT DO YOU WANT TO ACCOMPLISH THIS WEEK?

_____

_____

_____

_____

MEASURE, HOW ARE YOU GOING TO MEASURE YOUR ACCOMPLISHMENT(S)?

_____

_____

_____

_____

ACCOUNTABILITY, HOW WILL YOU HOLD YOURSELF ACCOUNTABLE?

_____

_____

_____

_____

ZEN-ZONE, DON'T FORGET YOUR ZEN.

_____

_____

_____

_____

Week 4

INFORMATION, WHAT ADDITIONAL INFORMATION OR RESOURCES DO YOU NEED TO GET TO YOUR NEXT STEP?

_____

_____

_____

_____

NOTEWORTHY, WHAT HAPPENED THIS WEEK THAT WARRANTS A JOURNAL ENTRY?

_____

_____

_____

_____

GRATITUDE, WHAT ARE YOU MOST GRATEFUL FOR TODAY?

_____

_____

_____

_____

"I believe everyone in the world is born with genius-level talent. Apply yourself to whatever you're genius at, and you can do anything in the world." —Jay-Z

MONTHLY
Reflection

- What were you amazed by the most this month?

- What was your biggest lesson this month?

- What do you plan to do differently next month?

- What do you need from your circle next month?

One word that best describes this month:

How will you rate this month?

Your Circle

Throughout my life, I've been told repeatedly, "You are the company you keep." Mostly, it was said by elders who were sharing wisdom earned through their own experiences. During silly seasons of my youth, I was too naive to understand the messages they were trying to convey about friendship. Now that I'm more seasoned, I've realized the significant impact our friends can have on our lives.

As we mature, we develop more social circles, including friends from work, virtual acquaintances, and members of various organizations. However, our inner circle is the core, consisting of people who share our interests and support us with genuine love. Some of these individuals may also be part of our social media groups, but our relationships with them extend far beyond virtual interactions.

Our inner circle may include family and friends who have been a part of our lives for so long that it feels strange to refer to them as just that. Still, they are the first people with whom we share our dreams, doubts, goals, and souls. They are our biggest cheerleaders and our safest vaults. Our inner circle is always there in times of need, and their opinions greatly influence our own.

Embarking on a journey of self-improvement can be a daunting task, as it involves a lot of uncertainty. However, having a supportive group of friends can make it easier to adapt to the transformation. Still, when we make changes that our friends do not understand, we may face some resistance. This is normal, since our friends are trusted accountability partners.

During your elevation, it is extremely important to pay attention to the people in your life. When a true friend offers constructive criticism, it should be followed by a solution or some other form of support. But if you have a friend who suddenly only criticizes you and their support is fleeting, it may be time to reevaluate your relationship with them.

Some people will never be able to accept you, exceeding the expectations they had of you. And it is best to discover that now before they start impacting the expectations that you have of yourself.

"Friends offer more than company; they help us carry out our calling."
—Dr. Dharius Daniels

"If you look at the people in your circle and you don't
get inspired, then you don't have a
circle. You have a cage."
--Nipsey Hussle

"Friendships between women, as any woman will tell you, are built of a thousand small kindnesses... swapped back and forth and over again."
--Michelle Obama

Week 5

ACCOMPLISH, WHAT DO YOU WANT TO ACCOMPLISH THIS WEEK?

_____
_____
_____
_____

MEASURE, HOW ARE YOU GOING TO MEASURE YOUR ACCOMPLISHMENT(S)?

_____
_____
_____
_____

ACCOUNTABILITY, HOW WILL YOU HOLD YOURSELF ACCOUNTABLE?

_____
_____
_____
_____

ZEN-ZONE, DON'T FORGET YOUR ZEN.

_____
_____
_____
_____

Week 5

INFORMATION, WHAT ADDITIONAL INFORMATION OR RESOURCES DO YOU
NEED TO GET TO YOUR NEXT STEP?

_____

_____

_____

_____

NOTEWORTHY, WHAT HAPPENED THIS WEEK THAT WARRANTS A JOURNAL
ENTRY?

_____

_____

_____

_____

GRATITUDE, WHAT ARE YOU MOST GRATEFUL FOR TODAY?

_____

_____

_____

_____

"The dream is free but the journey isn't."

—Bishop T.D. Jakes

Week 6

ACCOMPLISH, WHAT DO YOU WANT TO ACCOMPLISH THIS WEEK?

_____

_____

_____

_____

MEASURE, HOW ARE YOU GOING TO MEASURE YOUR ACCOMPLISHMENT(S)?

_____

_____

_____

_____

ACCOUNTABILITY, HOW WILL YOU HOLD YOURSELF ACCOUNTABLE?

_____

_____

_____

_____

ZEN-ZONE, DON'T FORGET YOUR ZEN.

_____

_____

_____

_____

Week 6

INFORMATION: WHAT ADDITIONAL INFORMATION OR RESOURCES DO YOU NEED TO GET TO YOUR NEXT STEP?

_____

_____

_____

_____

NOTEWORTHY, WHAT HAPPENED THIS WEEK THAT WARRANTS A JOURNAL ENTRY?

_____

_____

_____

_____

GRATITUDE, WHAT ARE YOU MOST GRATEFUL FOR TODAY?

_____

_____

_____

_____

"Have the courage to follow your heart and intuition. They somehow know what you truly want to become."

—Steve Jobs

Week 1

ACCOMPLISH, WHAT DO YOU WANT TO ACCOMPLISH THIS WEEK?

_____

_____

_____

_____

MEASURE, HOW ARE YOU GOING TO MEASURE YOUR ACCOMPLISHMENT(S)?

_____

_____

_____

_____

ACCOUNTABILITY, HOW WILL YOU HOLD YOURSELF ACCOUNTABLE?

_____

_____

_____

_____

ZEN-ZONE, DON'T FORGET YOUR ZEN.

_____

_____

_____

_____

Week 7

INFORMATION, WHAT ADDITIONAL INFORMATION OR RESOURCES DO YOU
NEED TO GET TO YOUR NEXT STEP?

_____

_____

_____

_____

NOTEWORTHY, WHAT HAPPENED THIS WEEK THAT WARRANTS A
JOURNAL ENTRY?

_____

_____

_____

_____

GRATITUDE, WHAT ARE YOU MOST GRATEFUL FOR TODAY?

_____

_____

_____

_____

"If all difficulties were known at the outset of a long journey,
most of us would never start out at all."

—Dan Rather

Week 8

ACCOMPLISH, WHAT DO YOU WANT TO ACCOMPLISH THIS WEEK?

_____

_____

_____

_____

MEASURE, HOW ARE YOU GOING TO MEASURE YOUR ACCOMPLISHMENT(S)?

_____

_____

_____

_____

ACCOUNTABILITY, HOW WILL YOU HOLD YOURSELF ACCOUNTABLE?

_____

_____

_____

_____

ZEN-ZONE, DON'T FORGET YOUR ZEN.

_____

_____

_____

_____

Week 8

INFORMATION, WHAT ADDITIONAL INFORMATION OR RESOURCES DO YOU NEED TO GET TO YOUR NEXT STEP?

_____

_____

_____

_____

NOTEWORTHY, WHAT HAPPENED THIS WEEK THAT WARRANTS A JOURNAL ENTRY?

_____

_____

_____

_____

GRATITUDE, WHAT ARE YOU MOST GRATEFUL FOR TODAY?

_____

_____

_____

_____

""We can always kind of be average and do what's normal. I'm not in this to do what's normal." —Kobe Bryant

MONTHLY
Reflection

- What was your most amazing memory this month?

_____

- What milestone(s) did you reach this month?

_____

- What do you plan to do differently next month?

_____

- What do you need from your circle next month?

_____

One word that best describes this month:

_____

How will you rate this month?   ☆☆☆☆☆

"The graveyard is the richest place on earth, because it is
here that you will find all the hopes and
dreams that were never fulfilled, the books that were
never written, the songs that were never
sung, the inventions that were never shared, the cures
that were never discovered, all because
someone was too afraid to take that first step, keep with
the problem, or determined to carry out
their dream."--Les Brown

Week 9

ACCOMPLISH, WHAT DO YOU WANT TO ACCOMPLISH THIS WEEK?

_____

_____

_____

_____

MEASURE, HOW ARE YOU GOING TO MEASURE YOUR ACCOMPLISHMENT(S)?

_____

_____

_____

_____

ACCOUNTABILITY, HOW WILL YOU HOLD YOURSELF ACCOUNTABLE?

_____

_____

_____

_____

ZEN-ZONE, DON'T FORGET YOUR ZEN.

_____

_____

_____

_____

Week 9

INFORMATION, WHAT ADDITIONAL INFORMATION OR RESOURCES DO YOU NEED TO GET TO YOUR NEXT STEP?

_____

_____

_____

_____

NOTEWORTHY, WHAT HAPPENED THIS WEEK THAT WARRANTS A JOURNAL ENTRY?

_____

_____

_____

_____

GRATITUDE, WHAT ARE YOU MOST GRATEFUL FOR TODAY?

_____

_____

_____

_____

"Time is more valuable than money. You can get more money, but you cannot get more time." —Jim Rohn

Week 10

ACCOMPLISH, WHAT DO YOU WANT TO ACCOMPLISH THIS WEEK?

_____

_____

_____

_____

MEASURE, HOW ARE YOU GOING TO MEASURE YOUR ACCOMPLISHMENT(S)?

_____

_____

_____

_____

ACCOUNTABILITY, HOW WILL YOU HOLD YOURSELF ACCOUNTABLE?

_____

_____

_____

_____

ZEN-ZONE, DON'T FORGET YOUR ZEN.

_____

_____

_____

_____

Week 10

INFORMATION, WHAT ADDITIONAL INFORMATION OR RESOURCES DO YOU NEED TO GET TO YOUR NEXT STEP?

_____

_____

_____

_____

NOTEWORTHY, WHAT HAPPENED THIS WEEK THAT WARRANTS A JOURNAL ENTRY?

_____

_____

_____

_____

GRATITUDE, WHAT ARE YOU MOST GRATEFUL FOR TODAY?

_____

_____

_____

_____

"Today was good. Today was fun. Tomorrow is another one."
—Dr. Suess

The Kaizen Effect

Kaizen is a Japanese term that refers to the practice of continuous improvement. Management theorists developed the philosophy during the Great Depression to boost wartime equipment production. Instead of making radical, expensive changes, manufacturers were advised to focus on small, incremental changes and improvements. The concept has since been widely adopted in various industries to promote ongoing progress and efficiency.

I was initially introduced to the Kaizen philosophy during school. While researching for one of my classes, I studied the auto manufacturer Toyota and learned about "The Toyota Way." This approach emphasizes continuous improvement and respect for people and still remains a core aspect of Toyota's strategies and accomplishments today.

A few years ago, I was reintroduced to the kaizen philosophy by Dr. Robert Maurer, a psychologist and expert in kaizen. In his book "One Small Step Can Change Your Life," Maurer explains how he used kaizen principles to achieve the same level of success as Toyota in his practice. He assisted his patients in achieving their objectives by managing the fight-or-flight response in their amygdala.

When we try to make significant changes and venture away from familiar territories, fear can often paralyze us. This happens because our brain's fight-or-flight response is triggered by newness. As a result, we tend to stick to what we know. It is not better for us, but it is known by us. To overcome this, Dr. Maurer suggested that his patients plan small, achievable goals to "tiptoe right past the amygdala," which is the part of the brain responsible for triggering the fight-or-flight response. By doing so, they could avoid fear and flight.

Dr. Maurer's book covers all of the principles, but I will only include the four that I find most useful.

1. **Ask small questions**. To identify possible solutions, ask yourself small questions. For example, if your goal is to save more money this year, one of your questions could be: "What small step can I take today to improve my financial life?

2. **Take small actions.** Now that you have identified one possible solution, it is time to figure out what small action you can take toward improvement. (Using the example from question one). One simple step that could be taken is to prepare coffee at home instead of stopping at Starbucks or Wawa. Another option is to bring your own lunch instead of eating out. Although these actions may appear insignificant, they can make a significant difference in your financial situation over time.

For example, I really dislike cleaning baseboards, but I hate seeing dust on them even more. So, instead of dedicating my entire weekend to cleaning with my Dyson and dust mop, I found a better solution. I would set a timer for 10 minutes and clean the baseboards in whatever room I was in. The following day, I would do the same thing. If I couldn't finish cleaning the baseboards during the 10 minutes, it didn't matter because I was done for the day. I would pick up where I left off until they were completely spotless. Eventually, I stopped using a timer and began using music instead. Before I knew it me, Beyonce, Jay-Z, and Kirk Franklin had cleaned the entire room, including the baseboards. To start, begin with a small change that won't overwhelm you but is big enough to eventually make a difference.

3. **Solve small problems**. It is best to solve minor problems while you have options instead of waiting until the problem is overwhelming and options are limited. So, if impulse spending was your problem, you could remove just one item from your physical or virtual cart before checkout. You could also leave your favorite credit card at home, virtually delete those that are saved on sites, and switch to spending cash for one day. When we physically spend our money, it has more of a psychological impact than the ease of using a credit or debit card.

4. **Eliminate waste**. Eliminating activities and costly habits that no longer add value to your life can help you save time and money. Time is a precious commodity that cannot be regained once lost, so it's important to be mindful of how you spend it. Therefore, it's a good idea to eliminate activities and even people who do not contribute positively to your life.

Amazing fact...

I chose my coach because his teaching philosophy of continuous improvement is based on Kaizen principles. It remains one of the best decisions I have ever made. ♡

*Notes: Maurer, R. (2014). One Small Step Can Change Your Life. Workman Publishing Company

"When life gets scary and difficult, we tend to look for solutions in places where it is easy or at least familiar to do so, and not in the dark, uncomfortable places where real solutions might lie... Fear is normal and a natural sign of ambition."

—Robert Maurer

Week 11

ACCOMPLISH, WHAT DO YOU WANT TO ACCOMPLISH THIS WEEK?

_____

_____

_____

_____

MEASURE, HOW ARE YOU GOING TO MEASURE YOUR ACCOMPLISHMENT(S)?

_____

_____

_____

_____

ACCOUNTABILITY, HOW WILL YOU HOLD YOURSELF ACCOUNTABLE?

_____

_____

_____

_____

ZEN-ZONE, DON'T FORGET YOUR ZEN.

_____

_____

_____

_____

Week 11

INFORMATION, WHAT ADDITIONAL INFORMATION OR RESOURCES DO YOU NEED TO GET TO YOUR NEXT STEP?

_____

_____

_____

_____

NOTEWORTHY, WHAT HAPPENED THIS WEEK THAT WARRANTS A JOURNAL ENTRY?

_____

_____

_____

_____

GRATITUDE, WHAT ARE YOU MOST GRATEFUL FOR TODAY?

_____

_____

_____

_____

"Remember, the same day we plant our seeds is not the same day we eat the fruit." —Tabitha Brown

Week 12

ACCOMPLISH, WHAT DO YOU WANT TO ACCOMPLISH THIS WEEK?

_____

_____

_____

_____

MEASURE, HOW ARE YOU GOING TO MEASURE YOUR ACCOMPLISHMENT(S)?

_____

_____

_____

_____

ACCOUNTABILITY, HOW WILL YOU HOLD YOURSELF ACCOUNTABLE?

_____

_____

_____

_____

ZEN-ZONE, DON'T FORGET YOUR ZEN.

_____

_____

_____

_____

Week 12

INFORMATION, WHAT ADDITIONAL INFORMATION OR RESOURCES DO YOU NEED TO GET TO YOUR NEXT STEP?

_____

_____

_____

_____

NOTEWORTHY, WHAT HAPPENED THIS WEEK THAT WARRANTS A JOURNAL ENTRY?

_____

_____

_____

_____

GRATITUDE, WHAT ARE YOU MOST GRATEFUL FOR TODAY?

_____

_____

_____

_____

"Start where you are. Use what you have. Do what you can."
—Arthur Ashe

Week 13

ACCOMPLISH, WHAT DO YOU WANT TO ACCOMPLISH THIS WEEK?

_____
_____
_____
_____

MEASURE, HOW ARE YOU GOING TO MEASURE YOUR ACCOMPLISHMENT(S)?

_____
_____
_____
_____

ACCOUNTABILITY, HOW WILL YOU HOLD YOURSELF ACCOUNTABLE?

_____
_____
_____
_____

ZEN-ZONE, DON'T FORGET YOUR ZEN.

_____
_____
_____
_____

Week 13

INFORMATION, WHAT ADDITIONAL INFORMATION OR RESOURCES DO YOU NEED TO GET TO YOUR NEXT STEP?

_____

_____

_____

_____

NOTEWORTHY, WHAT HAPPENED THIS WEEK THAT WARRANTS A JOURNAL ENTRY?

_____

_____

_____

_____

GRATITUDE, WHAT ARE YOU MOST GRATEFUL FOR TODAY?

_____

_____

_____

_____

"We can't become what we need to be by remaining what we are."

—Oprah Winfrey

Milestones Build Momentum

Breaking down goals into smaller, actionable steps is crucial for building momentum and reaching milestones. It is easy to become overwhelmed by the entire process if we focus solely on the big picture. Therefore, avoid self-inflicted delays and focus on the achievable steps that will take you closer to your goals.

Use milestones as guides with specific tasks and targets to direct your journey. Let's say you want to lose 4 pounds in a month. To achieve this, your first milestone should be to lose 1 pound every week. Did you know that there are approximately 3500 calories in one pound? So, to lose 1 pound a week, you need to cut down your daily caloric intake by 500 calories. There are numerous ways to achieve this, such as keeping a food diary, counting calories, eating healthier, exercising, etc. You can check out my website, dontforgetu.com, for additional resources on achieving your goals.

That was just one hypothetical way to break your vision down into steps, but your real journey should be filled with mile markers and roads of clarity. It's important to reach milestones as they help you keep track of your progress and provide a sense of momentum when you know you're on the right track. Even if you have to take some detours along the way, those diversions may lead to additional opportunities. And make sure that you celebrate reaching each of your milestones, no matter how small you think they are...it is a big deal.

MONTHLY
Reflection

- What was your most amazing memory this month?

_____

- What was the bravest thing that you did this month?

_____

- What do you plan to do for YOU next month?

_____

- What do you need from your circle next month?

_____

One word that best describes this month:

_____

How will you rate this month?   ☆☆☆☆☆

Week 14

ACCOMPLISH, WHAT DO YOU WANT TO ACCOMPLISH THIS WEEK?

_____

_____

_____

_____

MEASURE, HOW ARE YOU GOING TO MEASURE YOUR ACCOMPLISHMENT(S)?

_____

_____

_____

_____

ACCOUNTABILITY, HOW WILL YOU HOLD YOURSELF ACCOUNTABLE?

_____

_____

_____

_____

ZEN-ZONE, DON'T FORGET YOUR ZEN.

_____

_____

_____

_____

Week 14

INFORMATION, WHAT ADDITIONAL INFORMATION OR RESOURCES DO YOU NEED TO GET TO YOUR NEXT STEP?

_____

_____

_____

_____

NOTEWORTHY, WHAT HAPPENED THIS WEEK THAT WARRANTS A JOURNAL ENTRY?

_____

_____

_____

_____

GRATITUDE, WHAT ARE YOU MOST GRATEFUL FOR TODAY?

_____

_____

_____

_____

"Curiosity is the beginning of knowledge. Action is the beginning of change." —James Clear

Week 15

ACCOMPLISH, WHAT DO YOU WANT TO ACCOMPLISH THIS WEEK?

_____

_____

_____

_____

MEASURE, HOW ARE YOU GOING TO MEASURE YOUR ACCOMPLISHMENT(S)?

_____

_____

_____

_____

ACCOUNTABILITY, HOW WILL YOU HOLD YOURSELF ACCOUNTABLE?

_____

_____

_____

_____

ZEN-ZONE, DON'T FORGET YOUR ZEN.

_____

_____

_____

_____

Week 15

INFORMATION, WHAT ADDITIONAL INFORMATION OR RESOURCES DO YOU NEED TO GET TO YOUR NEXT STEP?

_____

_____

_____

_____

NOTEWORTHY, WHAT HAPPENED THIS WEEK THAT WARRANTS A JOURNAL ENTRY?

_____

_____

_____

_____

GRATITUDE, WHAT ARE YOU MOST GRATEFUL FOR TODAY?

_____

_____

_____

_____

"Whether you think you can, or you think you can't—you're right."

—Henry Ford

"Those times when you get up early and you work hard...when you stay up late and you work hard...when you don't feel like working, you're too tired, you don't want to push yourself, but you do it anyway. That is actually the dream...It's not the destination, it's the journey."—Kobe Bryant

Every Single Day
we have...

1,440 opportunities to do something to be better than we were yesterday for 1 minute.

144 opportunities to do something to be better than we were yesterday for 10 minutes.

96 opportunities to do something to be better than we were yesterday for 15 minutes.

48 opportunities to do something to be better than we were yesterday for 30 minutes.

24 opportunities to do something to be better than we were yesterday for 60 minutes.

"His mercies never come to an end; they are new every morning."
Lamentations 3:22-23

Week 16

ACCOMPLISH, WHAT DO YOU WANT TO ACCOMPLISH THIS WEEK?

_____
_____
_____
_____

MEASURE, HOW ARE YOU GOING TO MEASURE YOUR ACCOMPLISHMENT(S)?

_____
_____
_____
_____

ACCOUNTABILITY, HOW WILL YOU HOLD YOURSELF ACCOUNTABLE?

_____
_____
_____
_____

ZEN-ZONE, DON'T FORGET YOUR ZEN.

_____
_____
_____
_____

Week 16

INFORMATION, WHAT ADDITIONAL INFORMATION OR RESOURCES DO YOU NEED TO GET TO YOUR NEXT STEP?

_____

_____

_____

_____

NOTEWORTHY, WHAT HAPPENED THIS WEEK THAT WARRANTS A JOURNAL ENTRY?

_____

_____

_____

_____

GRATITUDE, WHAT ARE YOU MOST GRATEFUL FOR TODAY?

_____

_____

_____

_____

Stop finding the ways that you can't do something and find all the ways that you can and just go for it."

—Issa Rae

Week 17

ACCOMPLISH, WHAT DO YOU WANT TO ACCOMPLISH THIS WEEK?

_____

_____

_____

_____

MEASURE, HOW ARE YOU GOING TO MEASURE YOUR ACCOMPLISHMENT(S)?

_____

_____

_____

_____

ACCOUNTABILITY, HOW WILL YOU HOLD YOURSELF ACCOUNTABLE?

_____

_____

_____

_____

ZEN-ZONE, DON'T FORGET YOUR ZEN.

_____

_____

_____

_____

Week 17

INFORMATION, WHAT ADDITIONAL INFORMATION OR RESOURCES DO YOU NEED TO GET TO YOUR NEXT STEP?

_____

_____

_____

_____

NOTEWORTHY, WHAT HAPPENED THIS WEEK THAT WARRANTS A JOURNAL ENTRY?

_____

_____

_____

_____

GRATITUDE, WHAT ARE YOU MOST GRATEFUL FOR TODAY?

_____

_____

_____

_____

"The secret of change is to focus all of your energy not on fighting the old, but on building the new."—*Socrates*

MONTHLY

Reflection

- What was your most amazing memory this month?

_____

- What new resources did you use this month?

_____

- What are you going to do to celebrate YOU next month?

_____

- What do you need from your circle next month?

_____

One word that best describes this month:

_____

How will you rate this month?   ☆☆☆☆☆

"It is not the critic who counts;
not the man who points out how the strong man
stumbles,
or where the doer of deeds could have done them
better.
The credit belongs to the man who is actually in the
arena,
whose face is marred by dust and sweat and blood;
who strives valiantly;who errs,
who comes short again and again...
who at the best knows in the end the triumph of
high achievement, and who at the worst,
if he fails, at least fails while daring greatly."

—Teddy Roosevelt

Week 18

ACCOMPLISH, WHAT DO YOU WANT TO ACCOMPLISH THIS WEEK?

_____

_____

_____

_____

MEASURE, HOW ARE YOU GOING TO MEASURE YOUR ACCOMPLISHMENT(S)?

_____

_____

_____

_____

ACCOUNTABILITY, HOW WILL YOU HOLD YOURSELF ACCOUNTABLE?

_____

_____

_____

_____

ZEN-ZONE, DON'T FORGET YOUR ZEN.

_____

_____

_____

_____

Week 18

INFORMATION, WHAT ADDITIONAL INFORMATION OR RESOURCES DO YOU NEED TO GET TO YOUR NEXT STEP?

_____

_____

_____

_____

NOTEWORTHY, WHAT HAPPENED THIS WEEK THAT WARRANTS A JOURNAL ENTRY?

_____

_____

_____

_____

GRATITUDE, WHAT ARE YOU MOST GRATEFUL FOR TODAY?

_____

_____

_____

_____

"Self-discipline is when your conscience tells you to do something and you don't talk back." —W.K. Hope

Week 19

ACCOMPLISH, WHAT DO YOU WANT TO ACCOMPLISH THIS WEEK?

_____

_____

_____

_____

MEASURE, HOW ARE YOU GOING TO MEASURE YOUR ACCOMPLISHMENT(S)?

_____

_____

_____

_____

ACCOUNTABILITY, HOW WILL YOU HOLD YOURSELF ACCOUNTABLE?

_____

_____

_____

_____

ZEN-ZONE, DON'T FORGET YOUR ZEN.

_____

_____

_____

_____

Week 19

INFORMATION, WHAT ADDITIONAL INFORMATION OR RESOURCES DO YOU NEED TO GET TO YOUR NEXT STEP?

_____

_____

_____

_____

NOTEWORTHY, WHAT HAPPENED THIS WEEK THAT WARRANTS A JOURNAL ENTRY?

_____

_____

_____

_____

GRATITUDE, WHAT ARE YOU MOST GRATEFUL FOR TODAY?

_____

_____

_____

_____

"Every girl, no matter where she lives, deserves the opportunity to develop the promise inside of her."

—Michelle Obama

Week 20

ACCOMPLISH, WHAT DO YOU WANT TO ACCOMPLISH THIS WEEK?

_____

_____

_____

_____

MEASURE, HOW ARE YOU GOING TO MEASURE YOUR ACCOMPLISHMENT(S)?

_____

_____

_____

_____

ACCOUNTABILITY, HOW WILL YOU HOLD YOURSELF ACCOUNTABLE?

_____

_____

_____

_____

ZEN-ZONE, DON'T FORGET YOUR ZEN.

_____

_____

_____

_____

Week 20

INFORMATION, WHAT ADDITIONAL INFORMATION OR RESOURCES DO YOU NEED TO GET TO YOUR NEXT STEP?

_____

_____

_____

_____

NOTEWORTHY, WHAT HAPPENED THIS WEEK THAT WARRANTS A JOURNAL ENTRY?

_____

_____

_____

_____

GRATITUDE, WHAT ARE YOU MOST GRATEFUL FOR TODAY?

_____

_____

_____

_____

"There are no shortcuts to any place worth going."
—Beverly Sills

Week 21

ACCOMPLISH, WHAT DO YOU WANT TO ACCOMPLISH THIS WEEK?

_____

_____

_____

_____

MEASURE, HOW ARE YOU GOING TO MEASURE YOUR ACCOMPLISHMENT(S)?

_____

_____

_____

_____

ACCOUNTABILITY, HOW WILL YOU HOLD YOURSELF ACCOUNTABLE?

_____

_____

_____

_____

ZEN-ZONE, DON'T FORGET YOUR ZEN.

_____

_____

_____

_____

Week 21

INFORMATION, WHAT ADDITIONAL INFORMATION OR RESOURCES DO YOU NEED TO GET TO YOUR NEXT STEP?

_____

_____

_____

_____

NOTEWORTHY, WHAT HAPPENED THIS WEEK THAT WARRANTS A JOURNAL ENTRY?

_____

_____

_____

_____

GRATITUDE, WHAT ARE YOU MOST GRATEFUL FOR TODAY?

_____

_____

_____

_____

"At the center of bringing any dream into fruition is self-discipline."

—Will Smith

MONTHLY
Reflection

- What was your most amazing memory this month?

_____

- Were you satisfied with your progress this month?

_____

- What adjustments do you need to make next month?

_____

- What do you need from your circle next month?

_____

One word that best describes this month:

_____

How will you rate this month?

"Have dreams, but have goals. Life goals. Monthly goals. Yearly goals. Daily goals. I try to give myself a goal every day."

—Denzel Washington

Week 22

ACCOMPLISH, WHAT DO YOU WANT TO ACCOMPLISH THIS WEEK?

_____

_____

_____

_____

MEASURE, HOW ARE YOU GOING TO MEASURE YOUR ACCOMPLISHMENT(S)?

_____

_____

_____

_____

ACCOUNTABILITY, HOW WILL YOU HOLD YOURSELF ACCOUNTABLE?

_____

_____

_____

_____

ZEN-ZONE, DON'T FORGET YOUR ZEN.

_____

_____

_____

_____

Week 22

INFORMATION, WHAT ADDITIONAL INFORMATION OR RESOURCES DO YOU
NEED TO GET TO YOUR NEXT STEP?

_____

_____

_____

_____

NOTEWORTHY, WHAT HAPPENED THIS WEEK THAT WARRANTS A JOURNAL
ENTRY?

_____

_____

_____

_____

GRATITUDE, WHAT ARE YOU MOST GRATEFUL FOR TODAY?

_____

_____

_____

_____

"Be stronger than your excuses."

—Eric Thomas

Week 23

ACCOMPLISH, WHAT DO YOU WANT TO ACCOMPLISH THIS WEEK?

_____

_____

_____

_____

MEASURE, HOW ARE YOU GOING TO MEASURE YOUR ACCOMPLISHMENT(S)?

_____

_____

_____

_____

ACCOUNTABILITY, HOW WILL YOU HOLD YOURSELF ACCOUNTABLE?

_____

_____

_____

_____

ZEN-ZONE, DON'T FORGET YOUR ZEN.

_____

_____

_____

_____

Week 23

INFORMATION, WHAT ADDITIONAL INFORMATION OR RESOURCES DO YOU NEED TO GET TO YOUR NEXT STEP?

_____

_____

_____

_____

NOTEWORTHY, WHAT HAPPENED THIS WEEK THAT WARRANTS A JOURNAL ENTRY?

_____

_____

_____

_____

GRATITUDE, WHAT ARE YOU MOST GRATEFUL FOR TODAY?

_____

_____

_____

_____

"Some people want it to happen, some wish it would happen, others make it happen." —Michael Jordan

Week 24

ACCOMPLISH, WHAT DO YOU WANT TO ACCOMPLISH THIS WEEK?

_____

_____

_____

_____

MEASURE: HOW ARE YOU GOING TO MEASURE YOUR ACCOMPLISHMENT(S)?

_____

_____

_____

_____

ACCOUNTABILITY, HOW WILL YOU HOLD YOURSELF ACCOUNTABLE?

_____

_____

_____

_____

ZEN-ZONE, DON'T FORGET YOUR ZEN.

_____

_____

_____

_____

Week 24

INFORMATION, WHAT ADDITIONAL INFORMATION OR RESOURCES DO YOU NEED TO GET TO YOUR NEXT STEP?

_____

_____

_____

_____

NOTEWORTHY, WHAT HAPPENED THIS WEEK THAT WARRANTS A JOURNAL ENTRY?

_____

_____

_____

_____

GRATITUDE, WHAT ARE YOU MOST GRATEFUL FOR TODAY?

_____

_____

_____

_____

"Life is 10% what happens to you and 90% how you react to it."

—Charles R. Swindoll

Week 25

ACCOMPLISH, WHAT DO YOU WANT TO ACCOMPLISH THIS WEEK?

_____

_____

_____

_____

MEASURE, HOW ARE YOU GOING TO MEASURE YOUR ACCOMPLISHMENT(S)?

_____

_____

_____

_____

ACCOUNTABILITY, HOW WILL YOU HOLD YOURSELF ACCOUNTABLE?

_____

_____

_____

_____

ZEN-ZONE, DON'T FORGET YOUR ZEN.

_____

_____

_____

_____

Week 25

INFORMATION, WHAT ADDITIONAL INFORMATION OR RESOURCES DO YOU NEED TO GET TO YOUR NEXT STEP?

_____

_____

_____

_____

NOTEWORTHY, WHAT HAPPENED THIS WEEK THAT WARRANTS A JOURNAL ENTRY?

_____

_____

_____

_____

GRATITUDE, WHAT ARE YOU MOST GRATEFUL FOR TODAY?

_____

_____

_____

_____

"All you're going to lose is what was built for a person you no longer are."   —Brianna West

"Why" Check-In Time

Throughout your journey, there may be days when you question whether it's worth it. In those moments, use your "why" as motivation. Know who or what you're doing it for and how amazing you'll feel after achieving your goals. Above all, remember that your purpose is always worth the pain and the process.

- **W**ho or what are you doing it for.

- **H**ow amazing you are going to feel after you accomplish your goals.

- **Y**our purpose is worth the pain and the process.

"He who has a why to live for can bear almost any how."
— *Friedrich Nietzsche*

"Just do the work and the results will handle themselves." – Tony Gaskins

Week 26

ACCOMPLISH, WHAT DO YOU WANT TO ACCOMPLISH THIS WEEK?

_____

_____

_____

_____

MEASURE, HOW ARE YOU GOING TO MEASURE YOUR ACCOMPLISHMENT(S)?

_____

_____

_____

_____

ACCOUNTABILITY, HOW WILL YOU HOLD YOURSELF ACCOUNTABLE?

_____

_____

_____

_____

ZEN-ZONE, DON'T FORGET YOUR ZEN.

_____

_____

_____

_____

Week 26

INFORMATION, WHAT ADDITIONAL INFORMATION OR RESOURCES DO YOU NEED TO GET TO YOUR NEXT STEP?

_____

_____

_____

_____

NOTEWORTHY, WHAT HAPPENED THIS WEEK THAT WARRANTS A JOURNAL ENTRY?

_____

_____

_____

_____

GRATITUDE, WHAT ARE YOU MOST GRATEFUL FOR TODAY?

_____

_____

_____

_____

"An obstacle only emerges from a challenge if you succumb to it."

—Jurea Crudup

MONTHLY
Reflection

- What was your most amazing memory this month?

_____

- What did you learn about yourself this month?

_____

- What do you plan to learn next month?

_____

- What do you need from your circle next month?

_____

One word that best describes this month:

_____

How will you rate this month?   ☆☆☆☆☆

"The decisions you make today will determine the stories you tell tomorrow."

—Craig Groeschel

Week 27

ACCOMPLISH, WHAT DO YOU WANT TO ACCOMPLISH THIS WEEK?

_____

_____

_____

_____

MEASURE, HOW ARE YOU GOING TO MEASURE YOUR ACCOMPLISHMENT(S)?

_____

_____

_____

_____

ACCOUNTABILITY, HOW WILL YOU HOLD YOURSELF ACCOUNTABLE?

_____

_____

_____

_____

ZEN-ZONE, DON'T FORGET YOUR ZEN.

_____

_____

_____

_____

Week 27

INFORMATION, WHAT ADDITIONAL INFORMATION OR RESOURCES DO YOU NEED TO GET TO YOUR NEXT STEP?

_____

_____

_____

_____

NOTEWORTHY, WHAT HAPPENED THIS WEEK THAT WARRANTS A JOURNAL ENTRY?

_____

_____

_____

_____

GRATITUDE, WHAT ARE YOU MOST GRATEFUL FOR TODAY?

_____

_____

_____

_____

"We must never stop dreaming. Dreams provide nourishment for the soul, just as a meal does for the body."
—Paulo Coelho

Week 28

ACCOMPLISH, WHAT DO YOU WANT TO ACCOMPLISH THIS WEEK?

_____

_____

_____

_____

MEASURE, HOW ARE YOU GOING TO MEASURE YOUR ACCOMPLISHMENT(S)?

_____

_____

_____

_____

ACCOUNTABILITY, HOW WILL YOU HOLD YOURSELF ACCOUNTABLE?

_____

_____

_____

_____

ZEN-ZONE, DON'T FORGET YOUR ZEN.

_____

_____

_____

_____

Week 28

INFORMATION, WHAT ADDITIONAL INFORMATION OR RESOURCES DO YOU NEED TO GET TO YOUR NEXT STEP?

_____

_____

_____

_____

NOTEWORTHY, WHAT HAPPENED THIS WEEK THAT WARRANTS A JOURNAL ENTRY?

_____

_____

_____

_____

GRATITUDE, WHAT ARE YOU MOST GRATEFUL FOR TODAY?

_____

_____

_____

_____

"No one can make you feel inferior without your consent."
—Eleanor Roosevelt

Week 29

ACCOMPLISH, WHAT DO YOU WANT TO ACCOMPLISH THIS WEEK?

_____

_____

_____

_____

MEASURE, HOW ARE YOU GOING TO MEASURE YOUR ACCOMPLISHMENT(S)?

_____

_____

_____

_____

ACCOUNTABILITY, HOW WILL YOU HOLD YOURSELF ACCOUNTABLE?

_____

_____

_____

_____

ZEN-ZONE, DON'T FORGET YOUR ZEN.

_____

_____

_____

_____

Week 29

INFORMATION, WHAT ADDITIONAL INFORMATION OR RESOURCES DO YOU NEED TO GET TO YOUR NEXT STEP?

_____

_____

_____

_____

NOTEWORTHY, WHAT HAPPENED THIS WEEK THAT WARRANTS A JOURNAL ENTRY?

_____

_____

_____

_____

GRATITUDE, WHAT ARE YOU MOST GRATEFUL FOR TODAY?

_____

_____

_____

_____

"Nothing is impossible, the word itself says 'I'm possible.'"

—Audrey Hepburn

Week 30

ACCOMPLISH, WHAT DO YOU WANT TO ACCOMPLISH THIS WEEK?

_____

_____

_____

_____

MEASURE, HOW ARE YOU GOING TO MEASURE YOUR ACCOMPLISHMENT(S)?

_____

_____

_____

_____

ACCOUNTABILITY, HOW WILL YOU HOLD YOURSELF ACCOUNTABLE?

_____

_____

_____

_____

ZEN-ZONE, DON'T FORGET YOUR ZEN.

_____

_____

_____

_____

Week 30

INFORMATION, WHAT ADDITIONAL INFORMATION OR RESOURCES DO YOU NEED TO GET TO YOUR NEXT STEP?

_____

_____

_____

_____

NOTEWORTHY, WHAT HAPPENED THIS WEEK THAT WARRANTS A JOURNAL ENTRY?

_____

_____

_____

_____

GRATITUDE, WHAT ARE YOU MOST GRATEFUL FOR TODAY?

_____

_____

_____

_____

"Success is the sum of small efforts, repeated day in and day out."

—Robert Collier

MONTHLY
Reflection

- What was your most amazing memory this month?

- What will you leave behind this month?

- What do you plan to take with you into next month?

- What do you need from your circle next month?

One word that best describes this month:

How will you rate this month?   ☆☆☆☆☆

"God has equipped you to handle difficult things. In fact, He has already planted the seeds of discipline and self-control inside you. You just have to water those seeds with His Word to make them grow!"

Joyce Meyer

Week 31

ACCOMPLISH, WHAT DO YOU WANT TO ACCOMPLISH THIS WEEK?

_____

_____

_____

_____

MEASURE, HOW ARE YOU GOING TO MEASURE YOUR ACCOMPLISHMENT(S)?

_____

_____

_____

_____

ACCOUNTABILITY, HOW WILL YOU HOLD YOURSELF ACCOUNTABLE?

_____

_____

_____

_____

ZEN-ZONE, DON'T FORGET YOUR ZEN.

_____

_____

_____

_____

Week 31

INFORMATION, WHAT ADDITIONAL INFORMATION OR RESOURCES DO YOU NEED TO GET TO YOUR NEXT STEP?

_____

_____

_____

_____

NOTEWORTHY, WHAT HAPPENED THIS WEEK THAT WARRANTS A JOURNAL ENTRY?

_____

_____

_____

_____

GRATITUDE, WHAT ARE YOU MOST GRATEFUL FOR TODAY?

_____

_____

_____

_____

What you are seeking, is seeking you.

—Dennis Kimbro

Week 32

ACCOMPLISH, WHAT DO YOU WANT TO ACCOMPLISH THIS WEEK?

_____

_____

_____

_____

MEASURE, HOW ARE YOU GOING TO MEASURE YOUR ACCOMPLISHMENT(S)?

_____

_____

_____

_____

ACCOUNTABILITY, HOW WILL YOU HOLD YOURSELF ACCOUNTABLE?

_____

_____

_____

_____

ZEN-ZONE, DON'T FORGET YOUR ZEN.

_____

_____

_____

_____

Week 32

INFORMATION, WHAT ADDITIONAL INFORMATION OR RESOURCES DO YOU NEED TO GET TO YOUR NEXT STEP?

_____

_____

_____

_____

NOTEWORTHY, WHAT HAPPENED THIS WEEK THAT WARRANTS A JOURNAL ENTRY?

_____

_____

_____

_____

GRATITUDE, WHAT ARE YOU MOST GRATEFUL FOR TODAY?

_____

_____

_____

_____

"Change is painful, but nothing is as painful as staying stuck somewhere you don't belong."
—Mandy Hale

Week 33

ACCOMPLISH, WHAT DO YOU WANT TO ACCOMPLISH THIS WEEK?

_____

_____

_____

_____

MEASURE, HOW ARE YOU GOING TO MEASURE YOUR ACCOMPLISHMENT(S)?

_____

_____

_____

_____

ACCOUNTABILITY, HOW WILL YOU HOLD YOURSELF ACCOUNTABLE?

_____

_____

_____

_____

ZEN-ZONE, DON'T FORGET YOUR ZEN.

_____

_____

_____

_____

Week 33

INFORMATION, WHAT ADDITIONAL INFORMATION OR RESOURCES DO YOU NEED TO GET TO YOUR NEXT STEP?

_____
_____
_____
_____

NOTEWORTHY, WHAT HAPPENED THIS WEEK THAT WARRANTS A JOURNAL ENTRY?

_____
_____
_____
_____

GRATITUDE, WHAT ARE YOU MOST GRATEFUL FOR TODAY?

_____
_____
_____
_____

"To be yourself in a world that is constantly trying to make you something else is the greatest accomplishment."

—Ralph Waldo Emerson

Week 34

ACCOMPLISH, WHAT DO YOU WANT TO ACCOMPLISH THIS WEEK?

_____

_____

_____

_____

MEASURE, HOW ARE YOU GOING TO MEASURE YOUR ACCOMPLISHMENT(S)?

_____

_____

_____

_____

ACCOUNTABILITY, HOW WILL YOU HOLD YOURSELF ACCOUNTABLE?

_____

_____

_____

_____

ZEN-ZONE, DON'T FORGET YOUR ZEN.

_____

_____

_____

_____

Week 34

INFORMATION, WHAT ADDITIONAL INFORMATION OR RESOURCES DO YOU NEED TO GET TO YOUR NEXT STEP?

_____

_____

_____

_____

NOTEWORTHY, WHAT HAPPENED THIS WEEK THAT WARRANTS A JOURNAL ENTRY?

_____

_____

_____

_____

GRATITUDE, WHAT ARE YOU MOST GRATEFUL FOR TODAY?

_____

_____

_____

_____

"Empty pockets never held anyone back. Only empty heads and empty hearts can do that."

—Norman Vincent Peele

MONTHLY

Reflection

- What was your most amazing memory this month?

_____

- What was the most spontaneous thing you did this month?

_____

- What do you plan to do differently next month?

_____

- What do you need from your circle next month?

_____

One word that best describes this month:

_____

How will you rate this month? ☆☆☆☆☆

"Whatever the mind can conceive and believe, it can achieve."

Napoleon Hill

Week 35

ACCOMPLISH, WHAT DO YOU WANT TO ACCOMPLISH THIS WEEK?

_____

_____

_____

_____

MEASURE, HOW ARE YOU GOING TO MEASURE YOUR ACCOMPLISHMENT(S)?

_____

_____

_____

_____

ACCOUNTABILITY, HOW WILL YOU HOLD YOURSELF ACCOUNTABLE?

_____

_____

_____

_____

ZEN-ZONE, DON'T FORGET YOUR ZEN.

_____

_____

_____

_____

Week 35

INFORMATION, WHAT ADDITIONAL INFORMATION OR RESOURCES DO YOU NEED TO GET TO YOUR NEXT STEP?

_____

_____

_____

_____

NOTEWORTHY, WHAT HAPPENED THIS WEEK THAT WARRANTS A JOURNAL ENTRY?

_____

_____

_____

_____

GRATITUDE, WHAT ARE YOU MOST GRATEFUL FOR TODAY?

_____

_____

_____

_____

"Change is never easy, but always possible."

—Barack Obama

Week 36

ACCOMPLISH, WHAT DO YOU WANT TO ACCOMPLISH THIS WEEK?

_____

_____

_____

_____

MEASURE, HOW ARE YOU GOING TO MEASURE YOUR ACCOMPLISHMENT(S)?

_____

_____

_____

_____

ACCOUNTABILITY, HOW WILL YOU HOLD YOURSELF ACCOUNTABLE?

_____

_____

_____

_____

ZEN-ZONE, DON'T FORGET YOUR ZEN.

_____

_____

_____

_____

Week 36

INFORMATION, WHAT ADDITIONAL INFORMATION OR RESOURCES DO YOU NEED TO GET TO YOUR NEXT STEP?

_____

_____

_____

_____

NOTEWORTHY, WHAT HAPPENED THIS WEEK THAT WARRANTS A JOURNAL ENTRY?

_____

_____

_____

_____

GRATITUDE, WHAT ARE YOU MOST GRATEFUL FOR TODAY?

_____

_____

_____

_____

"If you prioritize yourself, you are going to save yourself."
—Gabrielle Union

Week 37

ACCOMPLISH, WHAT DO YOU WANT TO ACCOMPLISH THIS WEEK?

_____

_____

_____

_____

MEASURE, HOW ARE YOU GOING TO MEASURE YOUR ACCOMPLISHMENT(S)?

_____

_____

_____

_____

ACCOUNTABILITY, HOW WILL YOU HOLD YOURSELF ACCOUNTABLE?

_____

_____

_____

_____

ZEN-ZONE, DON'T FORGET YOUR ZEN.

_____

_____

_____

_____

Week 31

INFORMATION, WHAT ADDITIONAL INFORMATION OR RESOURCES DO YOU NEED TO GET TO YOUR NEXT STEP?

_____

_____

_____

_____

NOTEWORTHY, WHAT HAPPENED THIS WEEK THAT WARRANTS A JOURNAL ENTRY?

_____

_____

_____

_____

GRATITUDE, WHAT ARE YOU MOST GRATEFUL FOR TODAY?

_____

_____

_____

_____

"If your dream ain't bigger than you, there's a problem with your dream." —Deion Sanders

Week 38

ACCOMPLISH, WHAT DO YOU WANT TO ACCOMPLISH THIS WEEK?

_____

_____

_____

_____

MEASURE, HOW ARE YOU GOING TO MEASURE YOUR ACCOMPLISHMENT(S)?

_____

_____

_____

_____

ACCOUNTABILITY, HOW WILL YOU HOLD YOURSELF ACCOUNTABLE?

_____

_____

_____

_____

ZEN-ZONE, DON'T FORGET YOUR ZEN.

_____

_____

_____

_____

Week 38

INFORMATION, WHAT ADDITIONAL INFORMATION OR RESOURCES DO YOU
NEED TO GET TO YOUR NEXT STEP?

_____

_____

_____

_____

NOTEWORTHY, WHAT HAPPENED THIS WEEK THAT WARRANTS A JOURNAL
ENTRY?

_____

_____

_____

_____

GRATITUDE, WHAT ARE YOU MOST GRATEFUL FOR TODAY?

_____

_____

_____

_____

"Opportunities are like sunrises. If you wait too long, you miss
them."   —William Arthur Ward

Week 39

ACCOMPLISH, WHAT DO YOU WANT TO ACCOMPLISH THIS WEEK?

_____

_____

_____

_____

MEASURE, HOW ARE YOU GOING TO MEASURE YOUR ACCOMPLISHMENT(S)?

_____

_____

_____

_____

ACCOUNTABILITY, HOW WILL YOU HOLD YOURSELF ACCOUNTABLE?

_____

_____

_____

_____

ZEN-ZONE, DON'T FORGET YOUR ZEN.

_____

_____

_____

_____

Week 39

INFORMATION, WHAT ADDITIONAL INFORMATION OR RESOURCES DO YOU NEED TO GET TO YOUR NEXT STEP?

_____

_____

_____

_____

NOTEWORTHY, WHAT HAPPENED THIS WEEK THAT WARRANTS A JOURNAL ENTRY?

_____

_____

_____

_____

GRATITUDE, WHAT ARE YOU MOST GRATEFUL FOR TODAY?

_____

_____

_____

_____

"The future depends on what you do today."

—Mahatma Gandhi

MONTHLY

Reflection

- What was your most amazing memory this month?

_____

- Have you been a good steward of your time this month?

_____

- How will you encourage yourself next month?

_____

- What do you need from your circle next month?

_____

One word that best describes this month:

_____

How will you rate this month?   ☆☆☆☆☆

"Why" Check-In Time

Throughout your journey, there may be days when you question whether it's worth it. In those moments, use your "why" as motivation. Know who or what you're doing it for and how amazing you'll feel after achieving your goals. Above all, remember that your purpose is always worth the pain and the process.

- Who or what you are doing it for?

- How amazing you are going to feel after you accomplish your goals.

- Your purpose is worth the pain and the process.

> **"The goal is not simply for you to cross the finish line, but to see how many people you can inspire to run with you."**
> — *Simon Sinek*

Week 40

ACCOMPLISH, WHAT DO YOU WANT TO ACCOMPLISH THIS WEEK?

_____
_____
_____
_____

MEASURE, HOW ARE YOU GOING TO MEASURE YOUR ACCOMPLISHMENT(S)?

_____
_____
_____
_____

ACCOUNTABILITY, HOW WILL YOU HOLD YOURSELF ACCOUNTABLE?

_____
_____
_____
_____

ZEN-ZONE, DON'T FORGET YOUR ZEN.

_____
_____
_____
_____

Week 40

INFORMATION, WHAT ADDITIONAL INFORMATION OR RESOURCES DO YOU NEED TO GET TO YOUR NEXT STEP?

_____

_____

_____

_____

NOTEWORTHY, WHAT HAPPENED THIS WEEK THAT WARRANTS A JOURNAL ENTRY?

_____

_____

_____

_____

GRATITUDE, WHAT ARE YOU MOST GRATEFUL FOR TODAY?

_____

_____

_____

_____

"If a window of opportunity appears, don't pull down the shade."

—Tom Peters

"In the midst of chaos, there is also opportunity."

— Sun Tzu

"The future of life as we know it is being determined by everything we're doing—and not doing. Now."
Oprah Winfrey

Week 41

ACCOMPLISH, WHAT DO YOU WANT TO ACCOMPLISH THIS WEEK?

_____

_____

_____

_____

MEASURE, HOW ARE YOU GOING TO MEASURE YOUR ACCOMPLISHMENT(S)?

_____

_____

_____

_____

ACCOUNTABILITY, HOW WILL YOU HOLD YOURSELF ACCOUNTABLE?

_____

_____

_____

_____

ZEN-ZONE, DON'T FORGET YOUR ZEN.

_____

_____

_____

_____

Week 41

INFORMATION, WHAT ADDITIONAL INFORMATION OR RESOURCES DO YOU NEED TO GET TO YOUR NEXT STEP?

_____

_____

_____

_____

NOTEWORTHY, WHAT HAPPENED THIS WEEK THAT WARRANTS A JOURNAL ENTRY?

_____

_____

_____

_____

GRATITUDE, WHAT ARE YOU MOST GRATEFUL FOR TODAY?

_____

_____

_____

_____

"New beginnings are often disguised as painful endings."

—Lao Tzu

Week 42

ACCOMPLISH, WHAT DO YOU WANT TO ACCOMPLISH THIS WEEK?

_____

_____

_____

_____

MEASURE, HOW ARE YOU GOING TO MEASURE YOUR ACCOMPLISHMENT(S)?

_____

_____

_____

_____

ACCOUNTABILITY, HOW WILL YOU HOLD YOURSELF ACCOUNTABLE?

_____

_____

_____

_____

ZEN-ZONE, DON'T FORGET YOUR ZEN.

_____

_____

_____

_____

Week 42

INFORMATION, WHAT ADDITIONAL INFORMATION OR RESOURCES DO YOU NEED TO GET TO YOUR NEXT STEP?

_____
_____
_____
_____

NOTEWORTHY, WHAT HAPPENED THIS WEEK THAT WARRANTS A JOURNAL ENTRY?

_____
_____
_____
_____

GRATITUDE, WHAT ARE YOU MOST GRATEFUL FOR TODAY?

_____
_____
_____
_____

"One way to kill an opportunity is to avoid taking it."

—Jack Canfield

Week 43

ACCOMPLISH, WHAT DO YOU WANT TO ACCOMPLISH THIS WEEK?

_____

_____

_____

_____

MEASURE, HOW ARE YOU GOING TO MEASURE YOUR ACCOMPLISHMENT(S)?

_____

_____

_____

_____

ACCOUNTABILITY, HOW WILL YOU HOLD YOURSELF ACCOUNTABLE?

_____

_____

_____

_____

ZEN-ZONE, DON'T FORGET YOUR ZEN.

_____

_____

_____

_____

Week 43

INFORMATION, WHAT ADDITIONAL INFORMATION OR RESOURCES DO YOU NEED TO GET TO YOUR NEXT STEP?

_____
_____
_____
_____

NOTEWORTHY, WHAT HAPPENED THIS WEEK THAT WARRANTS A JOURNAL ENTRY?

_____
_____
_____
_____

GRATITUDE, WHAT ARE YOU MOST GRATEFUL FOR TODAY?

_____
_____
_____
_____

The key to life when it gets tough is to keep moving. Just keep moving."   —Tyler Perry

MONTHLY
Reflection

- What was your most amazing memory this month?

_____

- What were you most proud of this month?

_____

- What will you do to recognize YOU next month?

_____

- What do you need from your circle next month?

_____

One word that best describes this month:

_____

How will you rate this month?   ☆☆☆☆☆

"Working hard for something we don't care about is called stress. Working hard for something we love is called passion."

Simon Sinek

Week 44

ACCOMPLISH, WHAT DO YOU WANT TO ACCOMPLISH THIS WEEK?

_____

_____

_____

_____

MEASURE, HOW ARE YOU GOING TO MEASURE YOUR ACCOMPLISHMENT(S)?

_____

_____

_____

_____

ACCOUNTABILITY, HOW WILL YOU HOLD YOURSELF ACCOUNTABLE?

_____

_____

_____

_____

ZEN-ZONE, DON'T FORGET YOUR ZEN.

_____

_____

_____

_____

Week 44

INFORMATION, WHAT ADDITIONAL INFORMATION OR RESOURCES DO YOU
NEED TO GET TO YOUR NEXT STEP?

_____

_____

_____

_____

NOTEWORTHY, WHAT HAPPENED THIS WEEK THAT WARRANTS A JOURNAL
ENTRY?

_____

_____

_____

_____

GRATITUDE, WHAT ARE YOU MOST GRATEFUL FOR TODAY?

_____

_____

_____

_____

"Do what you were born to do. You just have to trust yourself."

—Beyoncé

Week 45

ACCOMPLISH, WHAT DO YOU WANT TO ACCOMPLISH THIS WEEK?

_____

_____

_____

_____

MEASURE, HOW ARE YOU GOING TO MEASURE YOUR ACCOMPLISHMENT(S)?

_____

_____

_____

_____

ACCOUNTABILITY, HOW WILL YOU HOLD YOURSELF ACCOUNTABLE?

_____

_____

_____

_____

ZEN-ZONE, DON'T FORGET YOUR ZEN.

_____

_____

_____

_____

Week 45

INFORMATION, WHAT ADDITIONAL INFORMATION OR RESOURCES DO YOU
NEED TO GET TO YOUR NEXT STEP?

_____

_____

_____

_____

NOTEWORTHY, WHAT HAPPENED THIS WEEK THAT WARRANTS A JOURNAL
ENTRY?

_____

_____

_____

_____

GRATITUDE, WHAT ARE YOU MOST GRATEFUL FOR TODAY?

_____

_____

_____

_____

"I think in life you should work on yourself until the day you die."

—Serena Williams

Week 46

ACCOMPLISH, WHAT DO YOU WANT TO ACCOMPLISH THIS WEEK?

_____

_____

_____

_____

MEASURE, HOW ARE YOU GOING TO MEASURE YOUR ACCOMPLISHMENT(S)?

_____

_____

_____

_____

ACCOUNTABILITY, HOW WILL YOU HOLD YOURSELF ACCOUNTABLE?

_____

_____

_____

_____

ZEN-ZONE, DON'T FORGET YOUR ZEN.

_____

_____

_____

_____

Week 46

INFORMATION, WHAT ADDITIONAL INFORMATION OR RESOURCES DO YOU NEED TO GET TO YOUR NEXT STEP?

_____

_____

_____

_____

NOTEWORTHY, WHAT HAPPENED THIS WEEK THAT WARRANTS A JOURNAL ENTRY?

_____

_____

_____

_____

GRATITUDE, WHAT ARE YOU MOST GRATEFUL FOR TODAY?

_____

_____

_____

_____

"Don't let your "self-talk" talk you out of what God has called you to do." —Craig Groeschel

Week 47

ACCOMPLISH, WHAT DO YOU WANT TO ACCOMPLISH THIS WEEK?

_____

_____

_____

_____

MEASURE, HOW ARE YOU GOING TO MEASURE YOUR ACCOMPLISHMENT(S)?

_____

_____

_____

_____

ACCOUNTABILITY, HOW WILL YOU HOLD YOURSELF ACCOUNTABLE?

_____

_____

_____

_____

ZEN-ZONE, DON'T FORGET YOUR ZEN.

_____

_____

_____

_____

Week 47

INFORMATION, WHAT ADDITIONAL INFORMATION OR RESOURCES DO YOU NEED TO GET TO YOUR NEXT STEP?

_____

_____

_____

_____

NOTEWORTHY, WHAT HAPPENED THIS WEEK THAT WARRANTS A JOURNAL ENTRY?

_____

_____

_____

_____

GRATITUDE, WHAT ARE YOU MOST GRATEFUL FOR TODAY?

_____

_____

_____

_____

"God made a way out of no way."

—Angela Bassett

MONTHLY
Reflection

- What was your most amazing memory this month?

_____

- What was the bravest thing that you did this month?

_____

- How will you guard your peace next month?

_____

- What do you need from your circle next month?

_____

One word that best describes this month:

_____

How will you rate this month?   ☆☆☆☆☆

"It was character that got us out of bed, commitment that moved us into action, and discipline that enabled us to follow through."

Zig Ziglar

Week 48

ACCOMPLISH, WHAT DO YOU WANT TO ACCOMPLISH THIS WEEK?

_____
_____
_____
_____

MEASURE, HOW ARE YOU GOING TO MEASURE YOUR ACCOMPLISHMENT(S)?

_____
_____
_____
_____

ACCOUNTABILITY, HOW WILL YOU HOLD YOURSELF ACCOUNTABLE?

_____
_____
_____
_____

ZEN-ZONE, DON'T FORGET YOUR ZEN.

_____
_____
_____
_____

Week 48

INFORMATION, WHAT ADDITIONAL INFORMATION OR RESOURCES DO YOU NEED TO GET TO YOUR NEXT STEP?

_____

_____

_____

_____

NOTEWORTHY, WHAT HAPPENED THIS WEEK THAT WARRANTS A JOURNAL ENTRY?

_____

_____

_____

_____

GRATITUDE, WHAT ARE YOU MOST GRATEFUL FOR TODAY?

_____

_____

_____

_____

"If you can't help me grow, there's no point with you being in my life." —Jill Scott

Week 49

ACCOMPLISH, WHAT DO YOU WANT TO ACCOMPLISH THIS WEEK?

_____
_____
_____
_____

MEASURE, HOW ARE YOU GOING TO MEASURE YOUR ACCOMPLISHMENT(S)?

_____
_____
_____
_____

ACCOUNTABILITY, HOW WILL YOU HOLD YOURSELF ACCOUNTABLE?

_____
_____
_____
_____

ZEN-ZONE, DON'T FORGET YOUR ZEN.

_____
_____
_____
_____

Week 49

INFORMATION, WHAT ADDITIONAL INFORMATION OR RESOURCES DO YOU NEED TO GET TO YOUR NEXT STEP?

_____

_____

_____

_____

NOTEWORTHY, WHAT HAPPENED THIS WEEK THAT WARRANTS A JOURNAL ENTRY?

_____

_____

_____

_____

GRATITUDE, WHAT ARE YOU MOST GRATEFUL FOR TODAY?

_____

_____

_____

_____

"Do not allow yesterday's garbage to influence your experience today. It is unnecessary to punish yourself for being human."

— Iyanla Vanzant

Week 50

ACCOMPLISH, WHAT DO YOU WANT TO ACCOMPLISH THIS WEEK?

_____

_____

_____

_____

MEASURE, HOW ARE YOU GOING TO MEASURE YOUR ACCOMPLISHMENT(S)?

_____

_____

_____

_____

ACCOUNTABILITY, HOW WILL YOU HOLD YOURSELF ACCOUNTABLE?

_____

_____

_____

_____

ZEN-ZONE, DON'T FORGET YOUR ZEN.

_____

_____

_____

_____

Week 50

INFORMATION, WHAT ADDITIONAL INFORMATION OR RESOURCES DO YOU
NEED TO GET TO YOUR NEXT STEP?

_____

_____

_____

_____

NOTEWORTHY, WHAT HAPPENED THIS WEEK THAT WARRANTS A JOURNAL
ENTRY?

_____

_____

_____

_____

GRATITUDE, WHAT ARE YOU MOST GRATEFUL FOR TODAY?

_____

_____

_____

_____

"You can't just sit there and wait for people to give you that golden
dream. You've got to get out there and make it happen for yourself."

—Diana Ross

Week 51

ACCOMPLISH, WHAT DO YOU WANT TO ACCOMPLISH THIS WEEK?

_____

_____

_____

_____

MEASURE, HOW ARE YOU GOING TO MEASURE YOUR ACCOMPLISHMENT(S)?

_____

_____

_____

_____

ACCOUNTABILITY, HOW WILL YOU HOLD YOURSELF ACCOUNTABLE?

_____

_____

_____

_____

ZEN-ZONE, DON'T FORGET YOUR ZEN.

_____

_____

_____

_____

Week 51

INFORMATION, WHAT ADDITIONAL INFORMATION OR RESOURCES DO YOU NEED TO GET TO YOUR NEXT STEP?

_____

_____

_____

_____

NOTEWORTHY, WHAT HAPPENED THIS WEEK THAT WARRANTS A JOURNAL ENTRY?

_____

_____

_____

_____

GRATITUDE, WHAT ARE YOU MOST GRATEFUL FOR TODAY?

_____

_____

_____

_____

"Consistency is an agreement you make with yourself to show up on the days when you feel tired, unmotivated, or tempted to give up. It's a personal obligation to invest in what produces the best ROI. Y-O-U!"   —Shanetta Davis

Week 52

ACCOMPLISH, WHAT DO YOU WANT TO ACCOMPLISH THIS WEEK?

_____

_____

_____

_____

MEASURE, HOW ARE YOU GOING TO MEASURE YOUR ACCOMPLISHMENT(S)?

_____

_____

_____

_____

ACCOUNTABILITY, HOW WILL YOU HOLD YOURSELF ACCOUNTABLE?

_____

_____

_____

_____

ZEN-ZONE, DON'T FORGET YOUR ZEN.

_____

_____

_____

_____

Week 52

INFORMATION, WHAT ADDITIONAL INFORMATION OR RESOURCES DO YOU NEED TO GET TO YOUR NEXT STEP?

_____

_____

_____

_____

NOTEWORTHY, WHAT HAPPENED THIS WEEK THAT WARRANTS A JOURNAL ENTRY?

_____

_____

_____

_____

GRATITUDE, WHAT ARE YOU MOST GRATEFUL FOR TODAY?

_____

_____

_____

_____

"To be amazing is to possess the power to ignite deep surprise and wonder, leaving a lasting impression."

—LaShon Fryer

MONTHLY

Reflection

- What was your most amazing memory this month?

_____

- What was the bravest thing that you did this month?

_____

- What do you plan to do for YOU next year?

_____

- What do you need from your circle next year?

_____

One word that best describes this project:

_____

How will you rate this month?   ☆☆☆☆☆

"Every great dream begins with a dreamer. Always remember, you have within you the strength, the patience, and the passion to reach for the stars to change the world." -Harriet Tubman

You are AMAZING!!

CONGRATULATIONS!

I am so proud of you, and I hope you are equally proud of yourself! This is an amazing accomplishment. Although your journey is not over, I hope you have discovered the resilience you didn't know you had lost.

Keep in touch and stay tuned for upcoming projects. Until then, remember that our gift will always make room for us, but we must also accommodate the gifts!

Stay safe, and don't forget to be amazing this year!

xo LaShon Fryer

Website: www. dontforgetu.com    beamazing@dontforgetu.com

Hello,
I'm LaShon

About Me...

I'm your go-to cheerleader for personal growth and self-sufficiency, and I'm totally aging myself by admitting that I have a whopping 15+ years of leadership experience under my belt! Even when I was green, my mission has always been to create a culture of development for my amazing teams. Think of me as a prisoner of optimism with a soft spot for Veterans and folks facing housing challenges. Just so you know, I'm also a Veteran, armed with an MBA in Non-Profit Management, and I'm currently holding down the fort on the East Coast!

"Being average is easy, but being amazing takes effort!"

Sagittarius

Fun Facts

- I love tacos!

- I worked at the Pentagon when I was in the Air Force.

- My favorite color is purple.

Website: dontforgetu.com

 beamazing@dontforgetu.com